"How to Get Over It in 21 Days!"

Messages and Lessons of Power, Hope, Faith, Motivation and Inspiration.

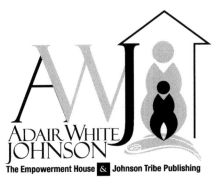

The Empowerment House & Johnson Tribe Publishing

Published by Johnson Tribe Publishing, LLC
Atlanta, GA

Johnson Tribe Publishing materials may be purchased for education, business, or promotional use. The author is also available for speaking engagements. For information, please contact us at (888) 400-7302, email us at info@johnsontribepublishing.com or visit us at www.johnsontribepublishing.com.

Manufactured in the United States of America
10 9 8 7 6 5 4 3 2 1

FIRST EDITION – July 2016
Creative Direction: Adair F. White-johnson, Ph.D.
Book Design: Stacey Bowers, August Pride, LLC
Photo Credit: Mistuh Will Photography
Makeup Artistry: Danielle Bessillieu

Library of Congress Catalog Card Number:
ISBN-13: 978-0-9977522-0-5
USA $12.95 • Canada $15.00

Dedication

This one is for ME.

When I write, I find strength in my own words and comfort in my release of my thoughts. Through my motivational messages, I inspire myself to continue to "push through the pain" and to follow the steps that God has ordered just for me. So this one, my eighth book, is dedicated to ME.

Introduction

Since my last book of inspirational messages, my life has been soooo busy. It has been filled with triumph, tragedy, purpose and perseverance but most importantly, it has been a "good life." You see, after my Dad's untimely and surprising death in November of 2013, the next two years were a challenge for me emotionally, psychologically, spiritually and financially. In all the ways that one feel can be broken, I felt the burden of each and every mode. My heart felt as though it were broken into a thousand pieces and I was unsure how to put it back together again. I still had dreams, but it felt as though those dreams were being deferred. I didn't want to go backward, but it felt like I needed to do this in order to find the strength to move forward. But that is the time that I began to lean more heavily on my triple shields of Grace, Faith, and Mercy. These shields became my armor of protection that led me as I climbed up mountains of despair, hurt, pain, fear, confusion and doubt. They also became my protection as I fought battles I couldn't see, wars that really didn't belong to me and as I became that foot soldier emerging through trenches in search of happiness and peace. And it was hard. It was tough. I kept telling myself "I may not be where I want to be, but I am not where I used to be" as a gentle reminder that every little step I took really was taking me in the direction I needed to go. I knew that every little drop eventually fills a bucket, so every movement I made brought me closer to the positive place that was truly my destiny. I was empowered knowing that leaning on my triple shields provided me with the strength I needed to push through my pain and follow along with the path that my God had created just for me. And, I was able to see the trail of happiness in my future so that all I needed to do was to "trust and believe."

This book shares with you the messages that I used to help myself through the most challenging times during this period. The words I share are reflective of the joy and pain that I experienced because of what was happening in my life. My words are raw and speak the truth from my heart because I hope to inspire you to move toward positive changes in your life. To learn how to "trust and believe" that if you lean on your triple shields of Grace, Faith and Mercy too, then you will find your happiness and peace within your life…despite and in spite of whatever you are going through at the moment.

"They," say it takes 21 days to break a habit and move towards positive changes, so this book has 21 days of motivational, and empowering messages that should inspire you to make the necessary uplifting changes in your life after each reading…Take it one day at a time and before you know it; you've made the change.

Enjoy…From my heart to yours.

Dr. Adair

Day 1

Some people spend their entire lives in search of their purpose.
Some people get lost in their struggle for significance.
And others wallow in a pond of confusion about the direction that their life should be headed in.

It can be so painful when you know that you are not doing what you want to do but are unsure about what you should be doing.

So you do the same thing.
Over and over again.
But you expect different results.
And you are never happy.

There are many people who feel "stuck" in their lives because they are just not confident about their next move.
And they think they don't have the strength to make it.

But you know what?
God has already equipped and empowered you with all of the tools you need to follow the steps that he has already ordered for you.

He has placed the passion, the purpose and the possibilities to prosper within your soul

You just have to believe.
You just have to be faithful.
And you just have to take the steps to "work a dream to live a dream."

You can't just sit there and expect your life to change on its own.
And you can't expect others to change it for you.

You own the power of change.
So use it.

Dreams never come with a warranty or guarantee so you can never expect that the dream you are living will last forever.
What about your next dream?
When you are finished with one dream, be prepared to receive, accept and live

the next one.

When I walked away from a six-figure income a few years ago to follow my next dream, I had no idea which path I would follow and my exact next steps that God had ordered for me.

But my Faith was stronger than my fear.

And I sustained the trials and tribulations of making my next dream come true.

You see, if we are not always dreaming of our next destiny point, then we are not living.
And if we are not thinking about the answers to our "What if?" questions then we are not breathing God's air.

Because every breath we take should be filled with the spirit of God's confidence in us.

We just have to believe.

Stop just sitting there and thinking about what should be doing.
And begin to create a plan to get it done.

Stop hoping and wishing for miracles in your life and begin making a new reality for it.

And stop just "putting it in God's hands" and walking away.
Because you were born with your own gloves to catch whatever God throws your way to make changes in your life.

Don't let your doubts destroy your determination.
Or let your confusion compromise your confidence.

Instead, allow yourself to learn.
Allow yourself the opportunity to believe in your dreams again.
And allow yourself to travel along the path that God has already created for you.

This is the only way that you will find a piece of mind.
This is the only way that you will be able to move beyond the "coulda, woulda, shoulda" in your life.

And the only true way that you will find happiness.

And yes, I already know that this is not easy.
I get it.
I understand.

But I also know that your Faith must be more powerful than any fear that you may have.
And then you can begin to push through all of your pain, allow yourself to heal from that pain, and give yourself permission to follow the dreams in your heart. Pain is not permanent so believe that your stumbling blocks will become your stepping stones to fulfill your dreams.

This is what will complete you and make you feel "whole" again.

This process does require that you "do the work" though and not expect it to be done for you.

You will see the passion in your purpose and will bring volume to the silenced voice of a dream deferred.
And you will be happy.

Yes, God is good.
But you can be a better you if you really trust and believe in his Word.

Lesson: Start doing the work.

Action for Change

List 2 things you need to change in your life today.

1. _____

_____

_____

_____

_____

_____

_____

_____

_____

2. _____

_____

_____

_____

_____

_____

_____

_____

_____

Day 2

Did you see play or movie "The Wiz?"

Watching "The Wiz" reminds of how many times that we forget what we are born with…

A heart to love.

A brain to teach us what we need to know to follow our dreams.

A portion of courage that allows our Faith to be stronger than our fear.

You see, God has already made us equipped and empowered.

He has already prepared us to be prosperous.

You see, there are so many of us sleeping with our dreams at night but living with nightmares during the day.

We are allowing the quadruple demons of the fear, confusion, doubt and failure to block the paths to our happiness.

We get caught up in "I shoulda, coulda, woulda" and do not focus on "I am, I can, I will, I do."

We allow those demons to paralyze our feelings of self-worth.

And we spend unnecessary time, energy and efforts in search of things that are already inside of us.

Looking for strength and power in all of the wrong places…

You see, when you were born, God had already given you everything you needed to be happy.

You already have the heart to love.

You already have the brain to figure it all out.

And you already have the courage to push through the pain.

Know that if you rely on the triple shields of Grace, Faith, and Mercy you don't have to exist in a living nightmare of unfulfilled dreams.

You can feel equipped and empowered that if you can "work a dream to live a dream."

I really believe that sometimes we are more fearful ourselves than we are of anyone or anything else because we are scared of our own dreams.

We are afraid our own destiny.

We are afraid to trust our own ambition.

And we don't allow ourselves to learn.

Instead, we allow ourselves just to wallow in self-doubt.

We allow ourselves to remain afraid of our own selves and not make changes in our lives.

We don't follow our dreams.

We don't walk along the path that takes us to a promising future.

And we don't follow the steps that God has ordered for us.

We just "get stuck" in stuff.

And that's why people are in the same place this year that they promised they would not be in the last year.

No real changes.

No real movement. Just because they get stuck.

Get out of your own way!

Start to plan.

Start to act.

Start to do.

Believe that you are all that God promised you to be because he has prepared you to be prosperous.

He gave you dreams, and he gave you the ability to fulfill those dreams, but it's your responsibility to get it done.

He already gave you the heart, the brain and the courage to make the difference in your own life.

You just have to believe.

And know that your name isn't "Dorothy," you don't have to "Ease on Down the Road" in search of a non-existent "Oz" to make your dreams come true.

Instead, trust and believe in the powers that you were born with.

Lesson: Don't forget what you are born with: A heart. A brain. Courage.

Action for Change

What does your Heart feel like right now?

_____

_____

_____

_____

_____

What are you thinking about right now?

_____

_____

_____

_____

_____

What are you afraid of right now?

_____

_____

_____

_____

_____

Day 3

There are so many of us sleeping with our dreams at night but living with nightmares during the day…

We are allowing the quadruple demons of the fear, confusion, doubt and failure to block our paths to happiness.

We get caught up in "I shoulda, coulda, woulda" and fail to focus on "I am, I can, I will, I do."

And we allow those negative demons to paralyze our feelings of self-worth.

But know that if you rely on the triple shields of Grace, Faith, and Mercy you don't have to exist in a living nightmare of unfulfilled dreams.

You can feel equipped and empowered that you can "work a dream to live a dream."

I really believe that sometimes we are more fearful ourselves than we are of anyone or anything else because we allow ourselves to hold us back.

We allow ourselves to wallow in self-doubt.
We enable ourselves to be okay with being to make changes in our lives.
We don't follow the true dreams in our hearts.
We don't walk along the path that guides us to promising futures.
And we don't follow the steps that God has ordered for us.

You see, we just "get stuck" in stuff.
Never becoming unglued.
And that's why people are in the same place this year that they promised they would not be in the last year.
No real changes.
No real movement.
Just because they get stuck.
Get out of your own way!
Start to plan.
Start to act.

Start to do.

And start to believe in your prayers.

Believe that you are all that God promised you to be because he has prepared you to be prosperous.

He gave you dreams, and he gave you the ability to fulfill those dreams, but it's your responsibility to get it done.

Never limit your possibilities by disabling your abilities.

Trust and believe that the dream is yours to fulfill and the nightmare does not belong to you.

Each waking hour is an opportunity.

And each fleeting moment is a possibility.

You only have a few moments in time at the exact time, to get it right, on time.

So just do it.

Know that the dream belongs to you.

It is yours to keep, and you should not allow anyone or anything to stop you from trying to reach it.

Dreams never come with a warranty or guarantee so you can never expect that the dream you are living will last forever.

When you are finished with one dream, be prepared to receive, accept and live the next one.

If you do, you will forever feel unfulfilled and will live a daily nightmare of life in wonderment.

Live your passion.
Live your purpose.
And live in peace.
That's the stuff good dreams are made of.

Lesson: Dreams are not just made for sleeping. Wake up and start fulfilling them!

Action for Change

My 3 Dreams today are:

1. _____

_____

_____

_____

_____

2. _____

_____

_____

_____

_____

3. _____

_____

_____

_____

_____

_____

Some situations in life are

MIND
OVER
MATTER

If you don't **"MIND"**, then it really should not **"MATTER."**

Lesson. Pick and choose your battles.

Sometimes I think that we just don't listen to the Word that God places in our hearts and in our lives.

Instead, we spend too much time trying to figure it all out ourselves.

We "want what we want when we want it," so we ignore the signs that God has placed in our lives to provide answers to our questions and give direction to our dreams.

I am not afraid to use my own life as an example for you to show that it can happen to all of us…

The year of 2014 was the worst for me because of the unfortunate, untimely and sudden death of my beloved father in late November 2013. My life was engulfed in despair that defined my life for the immediate six months following Daddy's death.

You see, during this time my life was stripped down to the bare essentials of life, and I operated at a loss emotionally, physically, psychologically and financially. Life basically "sucked" across the board for me and I didn't quite understand why and how everything could "hit" me at the same time.

I questioned God every day while begging and pleading for his Grace and Mercy to make things better. I thought I was listening to his Word when I would create action plans to move towards change. I knew that I leaned on my shield of Faith to simply allow me to rise out of bed daily to face all of the problems. And somehow I thought that just because I was a "believer" that everything would be "fixed" on my terms.

Wrong.

See, I was traveling on the right path that God had revealed to me; I was taking the right steps that he ordered for me, but I didn't listen to the Word that he sent to me.

I didn't hear him when he said: "Be still."
I wasn't paying attention when he said: "All is well."

I couldn't find the volume button when he said "Trust and Believe."

And I released the "pause" button while he was speaking about "Obedience."

13

Instead, I focused on making everything and everybody around me "okay."

I tried to fix it all myself while pretending that I was listening to God.

Wrong Again.

My God has been here all the while and was tryin' to tell me something.

Tryin' to tell me what I needed to hear.

If only I would listen.
How many of you are listening to His Word?
How many of you are hearing what he is saying to you?

Really?

You see, listening to what God is tryin' to tell you requires your undivided attention and obedience.

It is more than just nodding your head and agreeing---

It requires you to "Be Still" so that you can see the gifts that he has shared in your life.

So what if you no longer have the same job because of company workforce reductions?

You now have the gift to choose your next career!
So what if your heart is so broken, you can't find all the pieces again?
You own the gift of allowing someone else to love you!
So what if your spirit feels empty because you think you are missing a piece of it?
You now have the gift of filling it with God's presence!
And so what if you are afraid of what tomorrow may bring.
You now have the gift of learning how just to enjoy living in the moments of today.
See, I've learned that during this time of heartache and challenge my God was trying to tell me all along that I really needed to "Let Go and Let God."

He was trying to tell me that everything was already alright because I was traveling along the path he created for me, and he knows which direction I am headed.

He said that he never promised that my path would be a straight path and that there wouldn't be hills to climb, bushes to move out of the way and ditches that I may fall into while traveling. But he said he knew that I would always live in my purpose.

My God was telling me that despite and in spite of it all, my life was a good life, a thankful life, and a blessed life.

I know that sometimes we get caught up in things going on around us that we lose the connection of things going on inside of us. We stop trusting and believing in the voice that God has whispering in our hearts and our heads and begin to put our faith in what we can do and what others say.

But that won't work.
We have to listen.

We have to hear what God is trying to tell us --- that we may "bend, but we never break," that we may be "damaged but never destroyed" and that we be those foot soldiers emerging from the trenches, but our Faith is really our weapon of mass destruction.

We just have to listen.
We just have to believe.
Because God is ALWAYS tryin' to tell us something….

Lesson: What do you think God is tryin' to tell you today?

_____

_____

_____

_____

_____

_____

Day 5
"Broken"

I'm a broken woman.
Just a shadow of the person that I used to be.
And confused about who I want to become.I feel damaged.
I feel used.
And I feel unworthy.
Why?
All because of this thing called "Love."
So what do I do?
Hmmm….
Perhaps what I've always done…
Lean on my triple shields of Grace, Faith, and Mercy.
And be patient.
You see, I know how love hurts.
And I know the pain that I will suffer in order to "Get Over It," but I am willing to try.
I need to find "me" again.
So I can thrive and breathe again.
I am suffocating from my own heartache and pain…
My own asthmatic attack.
Hmmm….

Lesson: Know how you feel.

Action for Change

List three words to describe how you feel today.

1. _____

2. _____

3. _____

Sometimes people *love* you
the best way they know how

**But it's up to you to decide if you
will accept their type of love**

Lesson:
Know how you want to be loved

Day 6
"My Shields"

You know, I often write and speak about the three shields that I lean on daily for strength, guidance and direction. These shields of Grace, Faith, and Mercy have protected and covered me from all harm as long as I can remember. They work in tandem with each other and have never failed me yet. I want to share with you and example of how they have worked together in my life…I am living proof of the power they can have in your life.

Last year I was full of excitement and was so exuberant because one of my books made it to the top ten on the Amazon BestSeller List in its category… Actually, it made the BestSeller's List in three different categories. When I discovered this, I realized that a dream had come true…Once again, I proved my mantra correct "Work a dream to live a dream." My hard work and passion had paid off.

Since I was now a "BestSeller", I began to have new dreams about the future with writing and what I could do next….Never to be a girl who limits her possibilities and disables her abilities, I knew that I was ready to dream new dreams. I was grateful for my new BestSeller status, and I knew that I had Faith that my "time would come" because I was so patient in waiting for this day. But what about my Mercy and my Humility?

Hmmmm… My God made sure I remembered to cloak myself with those shields too

The same day I made the Bestseller's list I had to make a 10-hour road trip for family reasons. The trip had been planned for quite a while, and it wasn't a new venture for me. I thought I had mastered all of the "surprises" that may happen along the way, and the car was packed and prepared.

So we drove along, stopped a few places and the trip seemed to be "normal." When we arrived near our destination, we could not find a hotel to spend the night. We stopped at least 5 hotels, made several calls and searched the internet. Nothing. Absolutely. Nothing. Apparently there was a major event happening that weekend and coupled with canceled flights to several northern states (inclement weather) and passengers being stranded; all hotels were booked.

So we got back in the car at 1 a.m. and drove to further in hopes of finding a suitable hotel. We stopped, and I went into a hotel to check availability. No luck. I was weary, and I was tired with borderline frustration at this point after being behind the wheel for about 9 hours.

But, my God was ready to remind me that Mercy and Humility were my shields to lean on in this time of need. And I needed them now.

The young lady "Tanya" and the young man "Austin," who worked at our "final" hotel went out of their way to help us. Tanya called several hotels and searched the internet but also had no luck. Austin offered us the lobby couch, coffee and the use of the computer...Both quite aware of how "desperate" I was at this point. God knew that I was at their Mercy for a piece of mind at 2:15 in the morning. He sent me to a hotel that had workers who cared and would show Mercy towards me in my time of need. Although they did not have any available rooms and could not find one for me anywhere within an hour drive, they cared. When I said "I guess we will be sleeping in our car tonight," Tanya said, "Please use our parking lot. Park right here in the front where I can see you, and you can use our facilities whenever you need to." Have Mercy.

Me, my 13-year-old son and my 4-year-old niece spent the night in that hotel's parking lot.

A few hours later when I awakened and went into the hotel, Austin said, "Ms. Johnson, Good Morning! Breakfast will be served in a few minutes, please bring your family in and eat as much as you would like! No worries! You are our "guest."

Wow.

I was humbled because despite being a "Bestselling" author, I needed help with the basics of life. I was humbled because I was reminded that this shield protects me from becoming "too big" and warns me against forgetting "it's not what you have achieved" that makes you human. It's how you treat and respond to others that represent human actions. All that I have achieved in life did not matter to Austin and Tanya---they just saw a woman in need, and they responded to their call to action. For this, I am humble because despite and in spite of anything I already have, none of it mattered because, at that moment, I had none of it with me. Bestselling author or not, I was humbled to receive any assistance for my children and me at that moment.

You see folks, my shields of Grace, Faith, Mercy, and Humility are what I consistently lean on to know that everything is going to be alright. Through the horrible experience last night, I never grew hopeless...only tired. And never became truly frustrated...only perplexed. I knew then and always in my life, "Everything lil' thing is gonna be alright." I know this because I have my shields to lean on, to guide me and to protect me, and I never forget it.

Lesson: Even in the worst times of your life know that the "best is yet to come" and believe that it is really coming. Remember the shields in your own life and use then as your artillery in times when you are not sure what your next move will be. Knowing and doing this can only fulfill and strengthen you To be motivated, inspired and to be empowered.

What are your "shields" that you lean on?

Action for Change

List 3 shields:

1. _____

2. _____

3. _____

Day 7
#MyLifeMatters

Sometimes I forget that I really matter.

I get so caught up in doing everything for everyone that I don't do for myself.

You see, I get caught up in that "Superwoman" syndrome and focus on the things that I need to do, the things that I failed to do and the things that have to be done next.

And then fail to pay attention to me.

Is this you?

But you see, this is a problem because this means that we are not taking care of a child of God.

And that child is YOU.

We need to treat ourselves as we seek to treat others – with special care, dignity, and respect.

Pray for ourselves as we pray for ourselves.

Do for ourselves as we do for others.

#OurLivesMatter

Sometimes I feel like I am "Olivia Pope" because I try to "fix" everything.

And other moments I become "Claire Huxtable" providing stability and strength to all around me to turn obstacles in opportunities.

But even in these character models, I must remember that I am a child of God first and that he has entrusted me with myself to take care of me too.

Because my life matters.

I must remember that I need the sight of the blind man to really see the truth in my life.

I need the hearing of the deaf to listen to my heart.

And I need the strength of a paraplegic to walk consistently along the path that God has created just for me.

I should continue to lean of my shields of Grace, Faith, and Mercy to live my life through the eyes of Faith.

And not the eyes of fear.

I need to begin to see from the depth of my soul and understand that what I can see from the vision in my spirit will only make me better and stronger.

I should obey his orders to self-medicate myself with the power of his love because delayed obedience is really disobedience.

#MyLifeMatters

It is my job to take care of me.

I need to take care of this child of God.

I need to add my own name to my prayer list because I matter too.

And when I am "sick and tired," allow myself to be "sick and tired."

Because I deserve the rest.

I need to remind myself that no one can measure the strength of my soul unless they can do it from the depths of my stories untold.

And knowing that although my Faith is not absent of fear, I do not wallow in the mud patches of the doubt.

Because I am the foot soldier emerging from the trenches.

#MyLifeMatters

Give me permission to take care of me.

Allow me to fix my own life.

And take care of this vessel that God has given me to do the work he has assigned.

No excuses for loving myself.

No excuses for liking myself.

No excuses for believing in my dreams.

No excuses for working for my dreams.

No excuses for just being who I am.

No excuses for living in my purpose.

No excuses for living in my passion.

No excuses for embracing that I am already equipped and empowered.

No excuses for knowing that I have already been prepared to be prosperous.

Because I am a child of God and,

#MyLifeMatters

Lesson: Remember that you must first take care of you before you can really take care of anyone else.

Action for Change

Name 3 reasons why your life matters today:

1. _____

   _____

   _____

   _____

   _____

   _____

   _____

2. _____

   _____

   _____

   _____

   _____

   _____

   _____

3. _____

   _____

   _____

   _____

   _____

   _____

Day 8

"One Wing"

I hear the words of a song that said, "You cannot fly with one wing…" This song focuses on the fact that we can do a lot of things in our lives but just as a bird becomes paralyzed when it only has one wing, we can become paralyzed if we don't have a support network. It is up to us to decide who or what that support network will be.

For me, I decided a long time ago, that my shields of Grace, Faith and Mercy will always be my pillars of strength first, and then I will lean on my family and friends. You see, I am a lot of things in life, but I am nothing, absolutely nothing without my belief in the power of God in my life.

And I sometimes know it is hard to believe that God is still on our side when we have gone through so much…Life seems unfair, and you begin to think that you have been targeted. You think that the devil has taken over your life, and God is not touching your spirit. But you see, in reality, that is not true at all. God gives us what we need when we need it. He doesn't work on our timeline at all. You just have to keep believing that somehow and someway the heartache, the pain and any negativity in our lives will go away. It starts with your believing in God's presence in your life and that it is okay to ask for help.

Just because you ask for help does not mean that you are weak, it just means that you recognize that you cannot do it alone.

And you need someone or something to give you additional strength, guidance, direction and hope to get it done.

It means that you know that God has put you on this path and has ordered your steps, but he has also put positive people in your life to help you along the way.

You are not alone so do not think that you have to do it alone.

This is the part where you "Walk by Faith and not by Sight" and learn that along this path you do not have to allow the fear of failure to paralyze that faith.

You are reminded that you will never let your disabilities disable your abilities and limit your possibilities.

And you will know that you should not let your downfalls determine your destiny because your Dreams decide your destination.

Understand that sometimes there is power in pain.

And that pain can be a part of your power to "Let Go and Let God" in order to "fix it."

You see, suffering can lead to surrender, but it can also allow you to ask for help from your support network.

Because you cannot "fly on one wing."

We all need somebody.

We all need help.

And we all need the spirit of God in our lives to help us push through the pain and become those foot soldiers emerging from the trenches of despair, hurt, grief, and pain.

We need him to repair our wings so we can fly again and soar above the negative toxins and people in our lives so we can travel along that path he has carved for us in our lives to be all that we are destined to be.

We just have to ask for help because we can't "fly with one wing."

Lesson: Ask for help when you need it.

Action for Change

List 3 things that you need help with today.

1. _____

2. _____

3. _____

Name 2 people you can ask for help and they want to help you:

1. _____

2. _____

Day 9

"Peace Be Still"

Every possible Sunday that I can, I go to church to receive the Word of God. For whatever the reason it makes me feel better, stronger, wiser and more "ready" to face the world. On a particular Sunday the message I received from the Pastor resonated with my heart and soul, touched my core and really reached out to me.

My Pastor reminded me to allow "Peace Be Still" in my life and that I should not allow worries to "disturb my peace." He acknowledged that achieving daily "peace" can be a challenging feat but reassured me that if I really leaned on my triple shields of Grace, Faith, and Mercy, then I would not have to "stand on the battlefield" in combat with negativity daily. Recognizing, trusting and believing in God's Word will allow me to find the tranquility of my mind and the simplicity of my Spirit.

Hmmmmm....
Powerful stuff.
And yet, so very true.

You see, I already know that sometimes I bring my own drama to my peace, and I give in to the passion of anger, hurt and pain.

I get in my own way.
I need to stop blocking any blessings and allow myself to receive what is already mine.

Because what is for me, is for me.
And what is for you, is for you.
I already know that we spend an inordinate amount of time contemplating the good in our lives.

Questioning the peace.
We struggle for significance and never really allow ourselves to simply believe that greatness belongs to us.

Instead, we allow the fear, confusion and doubt to steer our emotional and psychological vessels into troubled waters.

We don't allow ourselves to sail along with God's navigation where we can float on positivity, prosperity and potential.

We just get in our own way.
Disturb our own peace.
And do not prepare ourselves for our purpose and become a trajectory toward triumph.

You see, if we keep holding up STOP signs along our own paths then how do we follow the steps that God has ordered for us?

If we keep planting more seeds of doubt, then how do we see that our Faith is stronger than our fear?

And if we keep things that do not allow us to become those foot soldiers emerging from the trenches, then how will we know that we are actually God's warriors of his Word?

How can we allow "Peace Be Still?"
Hmmmm….
We've got to get better.
We've got to move out of our own way and simply trust and believe in the plans that God has in store for us.

It may be scary.
It may be challenging.
It may be confusing.
And may even be lonely.
But knowing that we are on the road that was created just for us should equip and empower us to "get our minds right."

Knowing that the road we are on may be the path that is less traveled but it doesn't matter because we know that God is leading the way.

That's how we find peace.
That's how we discover our strength and reduce any weaknesses.
We can follow our dreams with passion and purpose when we know that God is on our side.

And we can work harder without a doubt when we know that we have a "piece" of mind.

We just need to get out of our own way and let God do his thing.

Just Trust and Believe.

Understand that "Peace Be Still," and then "Let Go and Let God."

Lesson: Sometimes life is just hard, and we have difficult choices and decisions to make. We get caught up in the fear, confusion and doubt, and we don't allow ourselves just to be still and feel the moment so we miss the "peace" that we can actually have. We try to figure it all out ourselves, and we question the answers that God has placed before us because it may not be the answer we like or want. But we have to stop that. We have to trust and believe that everything will be alright if we just follow along the path that God has carved out just for us. This journey will give us the Peace we need in our lives if we allow ourselves to learn. If we allow ourselves to accept. And if we allow ourselves to believe. Just start by getting out of your own way.

Action for Change

List 2 things that stop you from "getting out of your own way."

1. _____

_____

_____

_____

_____

_____

_____

_____

2. _____

_____

_____

_____

_____

_____

_____

_____

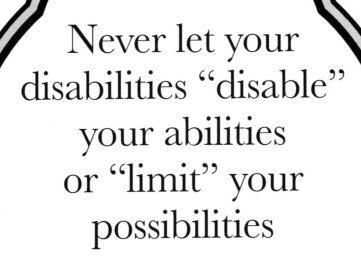

Never let your
disabilities "disable"
your abilities
or "limit" your
possibilities

Lesson:

*Just because you may have a
disability doesn't mean that your life
doesn't have infinite possibilities.*

Day 10

So tell me, what have you been "settling" for in your life?

Is it your job?

Your career?

Money?

A relationship?

Your dreams?

Hmmmmm…..

We are all guilty of "settling" at some point in our lives and I think we actually settle for something every day.

The questions become "What is it?" and "How long will we settle?"

I don't have the answer, but I know that at some stage in our lives we have to redefine what we want, what we need and what we think we cannot live without in our daily existence before we can make any concrete changes.

We convince ourselves that we are happy because we have 90% of what we want in life but if that 10% is potent and can destroy the 90% then that risk is just too high not to make changes.

I find myself often caught between "compromise" and "sacrifice" and not necessarily knowing when I've shifted positions and moved from one to the other.

I just realize that I am uncomfortable with the position that I am in, and I begin to feel the pangs of hurt within me.

I feel the pain of uncertainty and may begin to wallow in indecisiveness because of my doubt.

A confused mind does nothing.

So I begin to feel stuck.

But I deserve more.

I already know that I am equipped and empowered to do all the things that I am capable of.

And so much more.

But I just have to do it.

And stop settling because of my fear of the unknown.

My Faith has to become stronger than my fear.

And my confidence must overcome any confusion.

You see, because I already know that I am "so much" but I have to embrace that I am destined to be so much "more."

And in order to do that, I cannot settle.

Not settling requires extraordinary effort because we get comfortable in complacency, and it becomes easier to accept things as they are rather than do the work to make changes.

We need to create action plans that will help move towards change in our lives.

And if that means changing jobs, positions, relationships, and dreams.

Then so be it.

I really believe that if we put our power and our prayers into our passion then we can persist, persevere and prosper.

If we relinquish the right to settle then, we can reclaim the reason to be resilient.

It's like "mind over matter;" as much as we "mind" will be as much as it "matters."

We make our lives so difficult by wearing masks to cover our heartache, pain, bewilderment, fear, confusion, and doubt.

And then we forget to deal with these feelings.

And then we settle.

And we don't struggle for significance to make the difference in our lives.

But I can't do this anymore.

I am that foot soldier emerging from the trenches.

I am ready to lean on my triple shields of Grace, Faith, and Mercy for strength and guidance as I travel along this road that may be scary and a bit lonely.

Because I do not want to settle anymore.

I owe it my heart.
I owe it to my soul.
I owe it to my conscience.
I owe to the totality of who I am…the woman that God created.

I am.
I can.
I will.
I do.
I must.
Will we happy every day? I think not.

Will we ever get everything that we want in life and be 100% happy? Nope.
But I'm at the point in my life that I am willing to die trying.
Because I deserve more.
I want to be more.
And I am more.
And I'm not going to settle for less.
What about you? Are you still going to settle?

Lesson: At some point we have to make the choice about what is "compromise" and what is "sacrifice" in our lives to determine if we want to continue to "settle" for anything.

Action for Change

What are 2 compromises that you are making in your life right now?

1. _____

_____

_____

_____

2. _____

_____

_____

_____

What are 2 sacrifices that you are making in your life right now?

1. _____

_____

_____

_____

2. _____

_____

_____

_____

Are you willing to "settle" for any of the above? Yes_____ No _____

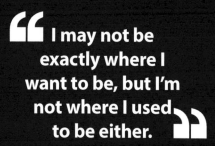

**I may not be
exactly where I
want to be, but I'm
not where I used
to be either.**

Lesson: Change begins with your perspective first.

Day 11

Sometimes we reach points in our lives when we feel trapped.

We feel as though we have gone as far as we can go but we still are not happy.

We want to go further, but we are just unsure about the direction we need to take next.

As though we are spinning in circles and getting nowhere.

And then we hurt.

We feel the pains of fear, confusion and doubt that cast shadows over us and blind us to the possibility of seeing a clear future.

So we sit, and we wallow in our hurt.

And we don't make any moves because we think that it is okay to accept life "as is" because things just are not "that bad."

But we are still miserable in our hearts.

When we are in our beds at night, and there are no distractions to our thoughts, we think about all that we "shoulda, coulda, woulda" done but simply did not.

And we wonder about the "what ifs?"

You see, we cannot continue to live our lives like that.

We have to find a way, to make a way, to discover the destination route to our dreams.

We need to create plans of actions that allow us to "work a dream to live a dream."

To prepare us for all of the possibilities.

And to use our pain as a birthing process for our purpose.

And allow ourselves to become equipped and empowered to emancipate ourselves from the mental slavery of fear, confusion and doubt.

It's hard.

Really hard to figure out what you sometimes want out of situations, things, and relationships.

But you just can't give up.

And you just can't give in.

You have to keep leaning on those triple shields of Grace, Faith, and Mercy to know that tomorrow is just a day away, so you have to keep believing that your dreams can become your reality.

If you really want them to.

And if you don't, believe that your shields will give you the strength to walk away.

Knowing that walking away doesn't mean that you have given up.

It just means that you have made a choice.

To make a choice you have to make a change.

And you must first change the way you think before you can change the way you behave.

Allow yourself to change and allow yourself to move forward.

I know it's tough, and sometimes we live in the fear of the unknown, spiral downward in confusion and deteriorate in doubt. But that has to stop.

Now.

Commit to excellence for yourself and your dreams.

Know that your steps have already been ordered.

Know that there is a path for you to travel on that was created just for you.

And what's for you, is only for you.

Break up your relationships with fear, confusion and doubt.

And deny any threats to your destiny.

Because you are already prepared to live in your purpose and prevail in prosperity.

It's already in you, but you have to decide what you are going to do.

I get it.

I understand it.

I know it.

I live it.

But I also believe it.

You just gotta do what you gotta do.

After all, your dreams depend on it.

Lesson: The only way to make a change is to make a change. Get Over It and start changing something, somewhere and somehow.

Action for Change

The change I will make today is:

_____

_____

_____

_____

_____

The change I will make tomorrow will be:

_____

_____

_____

_____

_____

These are the 3 changes I will work on this month:

1. _____

2. _____

3. _____

Day 12

The Resilient Woman

The Resilient woman knows that tomorrow is just a day away.

She understands that despite in spite of anything that happens today, tomorrow is just a day away.

The Resilient woman knows that she does not always have consult friends and family over decisions that she has to make.

She does not allow herself to be torn because she knows that God has already ordered her steps and that she leans on the shields of Grace, Faith, and Mercy to lead and guide her.

The Resilient woman knows that you must always "work a dream to live a dream" and when one dream is finished, you just start on the next one.

The Resilient woman knows that you must both love from your heart and your mind because a double vision is needed to coherently feel.

And she understands that sometimes you have to "walk away" and just because she "walks away" does not mean that she has "given up." It only means that she has only made a choice.

You see, the Resilient woman is actually that footsoldier emerging from the trenches ready to do battle ready to become that warrior of life.

She knows that her faith is stronger than her pain and that she should not be defined by her mistakes-- they are just things that she has done.

She is never sorry for who she is, just sorry but what she may have done.

She is not afraid to love and to be loved, but she also knows that some people love you the best way they know how.

But she also knows that she owns the power to determine if she is going to accept that love.

Yes, the Resilient woman is in touch with herself, so she feels her spirit in her choices, her decisions, and every breath that she takes each day.

The life of a Resilient woman is one that can include heartache and pain, but as she bounces back, she understands that despite and in spite of whatever it is that she has been through she can "Get Over It."

She knows that she can bounce back after hitting rock-bottom, she can hike up mountains while wearing stilettos and she can walk on tightropes without safety gear.

Just because she is Resilient.

You see, she doesn't need a superwoman cape either because she flies on the wings of hope, and she knows that when she's not moving, she's flying because she's got somewhere to go and something to do.

Knowing how and when to give herself and knowing when and how to forgive others is also a part of the Resilient woman.

She knows that "holding on and holding it in" is just like putting a Band-Aid on a gunshot wound. It will never heal, and it will only fester and infect the rest of her body and soul.

The Resilient woman knows that for each beginning there is always an end, and she knows, so she has to determine how and when to let things and people go. Most importantly, she knows when to "let go and let God."

Oh yes, the Resilient woman is so many things to so many people and most of all, she is the most important person to herself. She never allows herself to be more than what she really is and more than what God has determined her to be because she travels along the path that he is created for her to fulfill her dreams.

Grace. Hope. Humility. Determination. Intelligence. Gracious. Conscientious. Loving. Lovable. Competent. Diligent. Respectable. Smart. Ambitious.

Creative. A Dreamer.

And these are just the beginning of the adjectives that can be used to describe the Resilient woman.

She is living in her purpose, manifesting her destiny, and empowering her life so that it is Free! She is actively engaged in releasing any negative toxins from her life so she can only allow positive energy in her world.

Yes, the Resilient woman may be seen as an "omnipotent" woman to many, but she really is just she is living her life as God had planned her to be. the resilient woman is that you

And she understands that the word "No!" is actually a complete sentence, and it does not require a "Because" after it.

She's not afraid of ghosts of the past to haunt her future because her present is strong enough to determine what her future will be because her God orders her steps anyway.

Be sure to write in your journal today about what you think makes you a Resilient Woman.

Day 13

"Unpretty"

Sometimes we just feel "Unpretty" and we cannot explain it.

It is just a moment in time that we actually say "I woke up like this!"

And I am not even talking about the way we look physically.

I am not talking about having a "bad hair" day, or about our jeans fitting too tight on that day.

I am not referring to the big white pimple in the middle of our chin or the favorite sweater with the big stain on the front of it.

I'm talking about the little "demons" that exist within us that make us question our passion, question our purpose, question our existence and make us feel like we don't make a difference.

The voices that are in our heads that make us think that we are not "good" enough… that we are not "worthy" enough and that we are not "deserving" enough.

The thoughts that are resonating in our minds that make us feel that eternal happiness is being attacked. It's as though the core of our being is really a weapon of personal destruction.

The weight that we feel in our heart makes us feel that we are not strong enough to get through the day. That somehow we are not powerful enough to make the right decisions for ourselves.

That we are not resilient enough to just to bend and not break. To only feel a bit damaged and not totally destroyed.

You see, on those "Unpretty" days that we feel weak is when we think that we need our masks to cover up the pain, to shield the heartache, and to conceal our confusion.

And to be able to smile and pretend that we care.

We don't want the world to know how we really feel…that we are hurting inside and doubtful about the situation that we are living in.

And so we feel "Unpretty" by ourselves, and it is hard, and it is painful.

But!

If we remember to lean on our triple shields of Grace, Faith, and Mercy, then we will know that "this too shall pass."

And that "tomorrow is just a day away."

During that moment when we feel alone deserted, confused, unwanted, unloved, misunderstood, and in some cases depressed, we have to remember to keep the Faith to make it through the day.

We need to keep in mind that God doesn't put us through what he knows we cannot handle, and he has already ordered our steps.

We are just traveling along the road that he has paved for us.

Yes, I get it.
I understand.

I know it's hard, and I know it hurts because I've "been there I've done that" and I still go through it, but the only thing that keeps my chin up, and my eyes straight ahead is knowing that I belong to God, and I am walking along the road that was chosen just for me.

Allow yourself to feel.
Allow yourself to be.
Allow yourself to know that everything is going to be alright.
Because God is truly "on your side."
I am. I can. I will. I do.
Even if I am "Unpretty" today.

Lesson: Some days are just tougher than others….Get Over It, Get Through It and Keep it Moving! With God, Grace, Faith and Mercy on your side you will feel "Pretty" again.

Action for Change

Look in a mirror and tell yourself "I Feel Pretty" ten times. Do this three times today.

BE STILL.

Listen.

BE OBEDIENT.

God is always speaking to you. His volume never changes. His time is consistent, and his voice is electrifying. It's just the noise around you that deafens your ears to what he is saying.

Lesson: Silence the voice that interfere with God's message to you.

Day 14

"Just Talkin' to Myself"

What would you tell your 16-year-old self?

When I looked at a picture of myself at 16 years old, I have to chuckle because I remembered when the photo was taken. I remember that it was at my first job working at a bakery in Brooklyn. I would come directly after attending school and was responsible for serving customers, cleaning up and sometimes decorating the cakes.

There was a guy around who would sometimes come into the store, and he loved taking pictures so when he asked to take my photo, I did not hesitate. After all, he was a "regular" customer, so I didn't think taking a picture would do me any harm.

Fast forward 35+ years later and this picture speaks volumes about the center of my soul and the core of my existence because I see myself and the world differently now. I see such happiness, glow, innocence when I look at this picture. But I also see things in life now that I did not know actually existed at 16 years old, and these are the things I would teach my 16-year-old self:

1. **Life should not be full of "What If's?" Instead, ask yourself "Why Not?"**
If you live your life focusing on what "coulda, woulda, shoulda," then you may "never." Instead, dare to deliver your dreams. Walk down the paths of the unknown and begin to discover the depths of your destiny. By giving yourself permission to explore and examine, you are granting yourself the opportunity to dream.

2. **Allow yourself to learn.**
Yes, you may know some of it, but you do not know all of it. Allow yourself to engage in programmatic discourse, to recognize, understand and appreciate ideological stances that are in contrast to your own. Allowing yourself to do so permits you to expand your worldview, embrace your epistemological paradigm and become accepting of differences in life.

3. **Let your "No!" mean No and your "Yes!" mean Yes.**

Say what you mean and mean what you say. Do not waffle. While it is your prerogative to change your mind, you must be firm in the decisions that you make. That is the only way to stand firm in your convictions and never engage in a barter system of your core values and beliefs just for the love and acceptance of someone else.

4. Know your value and appreciate your worth.
Beyond money, know who you are and why you are worthy. You don't have to "give in" just to "get in." You need to find that healthy balance between compromise and sacrifice and still feel worthy. You don't have to give up who you are to be what someone else wants you to be. Ever.

5. Some people are going to love you the best way they know how.
And you are just going to have to determine if that is the love you need or if it is enough for you. Period.

6. Always lean on those triple shields of Grace, Faith, and Mercy.
There are no barriers to hurt, anger, frustration and betrayal in this world, so you have to create your artillery to help you get through it all. You cannot crumble just because your heart is broken and your ego shattered. You have to learn how to Get Over It…that requires leaning on these triple shields. No one or nothing can provide you with more strength than this armor of protection.

7. Get out of your own way.
Stop thinking so hard about your dreams and begin to work those dreams. Don't just talk about them, figure out how to do them…And then, just do it.

8. Everybody is not going to like you, & everyone will definitely not love you.
So what?

9. You own the power of change.
So stop complaining and change it.

10. Everyone who is sitting in your front row is not always clapping for you.
Scan the room to check everyone in your audience. Sometimes your biggest supporters are standing around the perimeter of the room. Don't be fooled by their "seat" in your life and don't automatically accept that if they are in the front row, they are supporting you.

11. Know that Love hurts.

As much as Love feels good, it has a tendency to feel bad too. You will have your heart broken in many different ways by many different people, and you may even do it yourself. But in the end, if you allow yourself to be loved, you will be loved in a way that you know is the right way.

12. Have an abortion. Several of them if necessary.

Terminate any pregnancy that will give birth to hopelessness, despair, disenfranchisement, negativity and toxins in your life. Anything that threatens to destroy your heart, mind, body, spirit and soul should be demolition. You will never, ever require those for positivity and success so abort them as quickly as you realize they are growing within you.

13. Be thankful. Be grateful. Be humble.

Never forget where you came from because that will help you to figure out the direction you are headed. But if you remain a believer, you will already know that God has ordered your steps, and you are just traveling along the road that he has created specifically for you, so you are humbled to know that you already have a personalized path in life. You should be grateful that you have already been promised prosperity, and you have been equipped and empowered to persevere and persist in your life passion.

14. Be still.

Sometimes you just have to sit and listen to your own heartbeat to hear its angelic sound. There will be times that you will be embroiled in the mundane daily activities of life and the trajectory of your goals that you may become confused about the tempo of your heart and what it means. Be still to know how to reacquaint yourself with the rhythm and beat again.

15. Be obedient.

As much as you will think that you are in control, never forget that God is really the one who holds the reins. There will be many times where you will have to "Let Go, and Let God." You will need to trust and believe in his Word and know that in places of turbulence and pain in your life, God is right there in you, next to you and with you. He will also be beside you as you walk along unfamiliar roads but you must be obedient to understand the clues and instructions that he leaves to help you navigate your life. This is how you will pass through any pain you may endure.

There are literally hundreds of other lessons that I could share and teach my 16-year-old self, but these are, by far, the most important 15 that I have learned since taking that picture 35+ years ago. I had no clue then about the woman I would become now and the lessons learned were actually blessings earned.

Knowing what I know now, I'm not sure if I would change much, but I do know that I wish I knew more then…Or, allowed myself to learn more. I know that I wish that I had allowed myself to be loved the way I deserved to be loved and then perhaps I could love a bit differently now. Sometimes, people just want to love you and sometimes you just have to let them.

Life's lessons often come full circle, and there are probably things that my 16-year-old self could teach my 50+year-old self right now, but I know that the core of my heart and soul has withstood the tragedies and triumphs over time. And for that, I am grateful. I am humbled, and I am thankful.

Lesson: What are 2 things you would say to your 16-year-old self?

Action for Change

1. _____

_____

_____

_____

_____

2. _____

_____

_____

_____

_____

Day 15

"Bag Lady"

I remember when I was about seven or eight years old when I first tried to run away from home.
I had just gotten in trouble with my mom and received a beating from her yet again, so I packed up my things into 2 brown shopping bags and said I was leaving.

I remember walking down the steps of my building, turning left, walking to the end of the block, turning right and then walking to the end of that street. I was headed to the train station in Brooklyn, and I already knew the way to get to my grandmother's house because we had taken that journey so many times before.

I also remember my mom's boyfriend, Mr. "Danny," followed me and tried to talk me out of running away, but I felt like I had no option. I couldn't listen to him because there was "no way" I could stay at "this place" where I didn't feel loved and appreciated.

So I decided to run. I decided that it was time to "go" -- it was time to run away.

It was time to run away from the heartache from the pain and from the emotional abuse and physical abuse that I experienced on a daily basis.

But I stopped at the end of the second street. I just stood there. I guess I knew in my heart that I really did not have any place to go and live. My dad lived in another country, and I wasn't sure if my grandmother would let me live with her "forever."

There was no place for me to go.
So I had to figure out my next steps.

Hmmmmm….

So here I was outside, down the street, at seven or eight years old with my worldly possessions in two brown shopping bags.

I didn't have a real plan.
I felt alone and as though no one understood my pain, and no one could make the pain go away because they didn't put it there.

Just confused.

Just hurt.
Standing outside with two brown shopping bags.

Now fast-forward to adult life—

How many times do we feel confused, hurt and as though we have no place to go? No place to "run and hide" from our pain?
We feel trapped. As though we are suffocating from our own pain and feel hollow inside as if our spirits have been ripped out from the heart.
How many times do we feel that the hurt is so bad that we want just to pack up our lives in two brown shopping bags and leave just to make the pain go away?

But we can't.
So we don't.
You see, that's the difference between being a child and being an adult.
As a child, we really believe we can run away, and the pain will go away once we are gone.

But as adults, we must learn that we have to push through the pain, develop action plans and steps that will guide us away from the pain.

We must begin leaning on those triplet shields of Grace, Faith and Mercy knowing that God will give us the strength we need to Get Over It.

You see, there have been many times my life where I have wanted just to pack up and leave with two brown bags. I just wanted to "go" and move to another life, a new mind space and a new emotional place where I would feel safe and loved.

But through the power of my prayer, I am reminded that sometimes there is power in pain because suffering can lead to surrender and then you are truly able to "Let go and Let God."

Your pain is a part of your power and through prayer, you can hear God telling you what to do, how to do it, when to do it, and who to do it with. It is the action plan that he has created for you and the steps he has ordered for you.

By trusting and believing "everything will be alright," I know that although it may hurt so bad right now, God has paved the road that I will travel to heal.

As an eight-year-old I didn't quite understand that so when I packed up those two brown shopping bags and walked down the street to catch the "A" train, I had no idea how the power of prayer really works.

I do now.

Lesson: Before you pack those brown bags and try to run from your pain, remember that God is here for you. He will give you what you need to push through the pain, and will remind you that you always have those triple shields of Grace, Faith, and Mercy.

Action for Change

List one thing that you are trying to run away from in your life:

_____

_____

_____

_____

_____

_____

_____

_____

_____

_____

_____

_____

_____

_____

_____

_____

Day 16

Yesterday I went to the gym….Like thousands of other people, I vowed to get "fit", and my visit to the gym was "proof" that I was serious about this commitment.

Hmmmm….

As I huffed, puffed and struggled on the treadmill with the trainer "barking" commands over the loud and busy music that was supposed to motivate us, I found myself drifting off into my own thoughts…

I thought about how ridiculous this "commitment," I made was….Heck, I only wear a size 2 so what was I doing there? I didn't need to burn any calories, and I am definitely not overweight.

I thought about how hard something as simple as walking could be when you are not walking down your normal path.

And I thought about giving up. Leaving that gym and never going back.

All because it was hard.

Hmmmm….

Isn't this parallel to many things in our lives? When faced with adversity and challenges don't we want just to give up and convince ourselves that we don't need to do it?

Well, I honestly believe that if we continue to do that, our dreams will never come true…If we just stop because we are uncomfortable, tired and "sweating" then how will we accomplish our goals?

Sometimes the greatest things in life, that we decided we want, are the things in life that cost us the most emotionally, physically and psychologically. These are the things that require us to give up and give into our hearts and souls. And these are the elements of our lives that can rape us of the dreams we have if we don't work from the core of our existence.

And I know that it is hard to keep climbing up a hill in flip flops…We keep feeling as though we are backsliding…And maybe sometimes we are. But know that for every three feet that we go backward we can leap five feet forward. Know that our Faith propelled us to our own level of greatness, and that same Faith is stronger than our pain and our weaknesses.

New things are always a bit challenging for me because I feel as though I have to commit to a "resolution" as sort of a plan for the year, and I never know what I want to commit to. I decided this year to create an "Action Plan" to lead and guide me throughout the year. The difference this year, however, is that I am praying about it all. I am talking about my God and listening for a response because I know that he orders my steps…While writing my action plan and the steps, I am stopping and thinking about how my Faith fits all of this….This is new for me this year….It is a different perspective.

Lesson: Be sure to write in your journal about a new perspective you would like to have about a situation in your life.

If you keep thinking it, eventually you will **BELIEVE** it.

If you keep saying it, eventually someone else will **HEAR** it.

But if you keep doing it, them it becomes reality and everyone will **SEE** it.

**Lesson. Think It . Say. It Do It.
That's the only way dreams some true.**

"You Never Know…"

I was feeling a bit nostalgic last week when I found an old college ID in a drawer while searching for AAA batteries…It made me think back in time when I was full of dreams and praying for endless opportunities that would help make those dreams come true. I started thinking about how we just don't know where life is going to take us…We just don't know….

When I was a sixteen-year-old freshman attending Daemen College in Amherst, New York I had no idea how my life would change because of that experience. You see, I was admitted to college on a "wing and a prayer." Having barely completed high school because of lack of effort and the negative influence of a home environment I just didn't have a clue about how my life would turn out. What I did know, however, was that I had a dream that this was my opportunity to make it come true.

My life did not begin as it is now; there was an abundance of hurt and pain. I was twelve the first time I tried to commit suicide. It was right after I had been beaten with belts and broomsticks by my mother and her boyfriend in the back storage room of the liquor store they owned and operated. Why was I beaten? Because I went to the library with my friends and my mother didn't believe me…she thought I was lying and sneaking around with boys. I didn't even know how to sneak around at that point! So she beat me and tried to beat me some more in hopes of getting a confession out of me. And then she had her boyfriend and beat me. I had lumps on my legs from the broomsticks and jumping over the boxes in the storage room and falling to the floor. This time, it felt like it was "one beating too many." When they finally released me and allowed me to go home, I just wanted to be "free." I needed to feel numb because it was one thing to be beaten when you are wrong but quite another to receive such a brutal beating when you have done nothing wrong. I knew that if I could go to live in a "better place" then God would take care of me.

That afternoon I took 13 Tylenol pills along with a couple of drinks from my mom's vodka bottle that she kept hidden under the cushion of the couch that she slept on. I remember falling asleep on that couch shortly after taking the pills but awakening to the sound of the phone ringing persistently. It was one of those old rotary phones, and it was in the hallway of the apartment so we kept the ringer up loud so we could hear it from all rooms.

Rinnggggg….rinnnggggg…rinnnggggg…. the shrilling sound was pulsating in my ears, and I was awakened…I got up to answer the phone, and it was my mom, and then I realized "Damn, I am still alive."

During this time in my life, I barely existed. I got up, and I functioned with a smile on my face so no one could see the pain within. I knew it didn't feel right but these were my own demons, and no one else had to know about them…I just knew I had to find a place in my life where I could follow my dreams and become that person that I knew God planned for me to be.

You see, I grew up in economic poverty in Brooklyn, and it was often assumed that I grew up in intellectual poverty as well. My dad lived in another country so I was basically raised in a single-parent household living below the poverty line with an alcoholic, abusive mother and I shouldn't have "made it." The statistical odds were against me, but I refused to let those odds determine my fate. I believed that there were already enough odds stacked up against me from my own family history and background, so I couldn't let stats determine my next steps.

We were probably the poorest family on the block where we lived. At least, it felt like it because we lived among filth because my grandmother was elderly, physically limited and my mother simply ignored the dirt. So we lived in this two bedroom apartment with the roaches and mice. When you walked into the kitchen at night, you would have to stomp on the kitchen floor to scare the mice and make the roaches scatter. You couldn't leave any food on the counter because the mice would come out and eat the food. In fact, that's how I learned that mice loved chocolate! I brought home a box of chocolate bars from school to sell as a part of a fundraiser, and I left the box on the counter. The next morning I discovered the mice had eaten through the box, the paper and the foil that covered the chocolate bars. The entire $30 box was ruined, and I was too embarrassed to explain to my teacher what happened to the chocolate bars so the $30 debt remained on my record until I was scheduled to graduate four years later and my uncle paid the fee so I could receive my high school diploma. That was my life. Those were my odds.

The heat never worked right either, and it was never warm enough in the apartment. I remember my grandmother used to turn the oven on and close the dining room door so we could have heat back there. We would pile up in that back room to stay warm, and we were afraid to get up to go to the bathroom in the middle of the night it was just too cold. You could actually see your breath when you blew outward; it was that cold in the apartment. I used to sit on the radiators throughout the day while in junior high school because I thought that if I saved enough heat in my body from school then somehow I would be warmer at home.

I didn't have a bed, and I slept on the floor with my grandmother. She made pallets, and we used to snuggle up right next to each other to be warm. I remember her having a tapestry with a picture of Jesus on it that belonged on the wall which she took down because it was sooooo heavy and she knew it would keep us warm. We slept under that tapestry on the floor for many years…just to keep warm and be protected by Jesus. And that's when I began just to think…and dream some more about how I could overcome my own odds. How could I rise up and fly away to find my own stars amid the pitch black night sky?

What did I need to do to fulfill my own dreams and beat those statistics that had spoken volumes for my so-called silenced future? What could I do to push through the pain and ease the throbbing that I felt inside of me so that I could feel warm, safe and protected? I knew that a change had to be in the forecast for me, and it had to be a positive change so that I could follow my dreams.

When my mom died of alcoholism at the age of 37, and I was only 14, I figured that there wasn't anything worse that could happen to me from that point on. I convinced myself that the "hole" in my heart was so deep that no one else in the world would be allowed to hurt me that way. I knew that if I could "get over" my mom's death, then there wouldn't be any other hurt that I couldn't get over for the rest of my life, so I used that pain as the armored truck to combat future suffrage.

I was failing in school at the time of her death, but I also knew that I had to get over myself and overcome my own odds to become a future success. I used my own life experience as my motivation and inspiration because I knew the emotional and psychological state of mind that I was left in after my mom died. Yes, I was a victim of physical, emotional, psychological and sexual abuse under her watch but she was still my mother, and I loved her. I had to become that foot soldier emerging from those trenches of disparity to defy these odds, and it didn't matter what statistics noted because those numbers didn't live with me daily. Feelings of heartache, loneliness, emptiness, sorrow and shame had taken residence in my life, and it didn't feel good. But when I went away to Daemen College, that made the difference in my life.

I arrived at this small, quaint, former Catholic college and I immediately felt safe and supported. It was an atmosphere that cultivated and encouraged my dreams so that I could "be somebody." I inhaled all the positivity during that time and exhaled anything that was an obstacle to my opportunity. I was living in my purpose, persevering in my passion and preparing for my prosperity… and I was only sixteen years old when it all began.

You see, it doesn't begin with age. It doesn't begin with race, class, gender and socioeconomic status. It begins with you. It begins with the mindset that you learn to master. It begins with recognizing and knowing that you should never allow your disabilities to disable your abilities or limit your possibilities. Don't make excuses, make adjustments. And when you do this, you just never know what will happen.

I made the decision to wrap my arms all things positive and purposeful in my life; this included social, emotional, academic and spiritual things and people. I found all of this on the campus, and I worked hard. I mapped out the course I needed to follow to complete my degree and with support, I did that within 3 ½ years. Imagine that? The kid who arrived on campus with lackluster high school grades was now graduating a semester early and moving on to graduate school. Now, that is an example of overcoming your odds, working your dream to live your dream and trusting and believing in the path that God had created just for you. Traveling along that road that he paved for your unique steps. If I didn't have Faith that "every lil' thing would be alright," I wouldn't have made it because the odds were stacked so high against me.

But let me tell you, I didn't know that my story could make a difference in the lives of others. I didn't know that my struggles could be significant for someone else. And I didn't know that the power of my perseverance could prepare others for the journey that they were about to take. But Daemen College knew, and they invested in my story.

On September 10, 2015, the skinny lil' kid from Brooklyn delivered the keynote speech to over 500 people at the Convocation ceremony at Daemen

College. The very college where she stepped onto the campus 30+ years earlier as a scared, confused, lonely but determined young girl. Her life had been drastically changed because of her collegiate experience, and she was there to motivate, empower and inspire the freshman class, faculty, staff and her former professor. She delivered a message that focused on the question "What If?" because she wanted to remind them of life's infinite possibilities and what you could do if you just trust and believe.

As a young girl, I just didn't know. I didn't know what my life would eventually look like, feel like and just "be." All that I did know was that I had dreams and despite and in spite of anything that I had previously been through in my life, I was determined to make those dreams come true. I say to you that you must be that foot soldier trudging through the trenches to embrace your dreams. When someone gives you an opportunity, take it and make it a reality. Don't walk away from challenges, face them because you are already equipped and empowered to persevere through pain. You just have to want it. You have to feel it. You have to need it. Knowing this can help you create your action plans to move toward positive changes. You just never know what tomorrow will bring but always understand that tomorrow is just a day away, so just allow yourself to become prepared. Allow yourself to learn. Allow yourself to know. And allow yourself to continue to dream. And when one dreams is fulfilled, start working on the next one because dreams are not just made for sleeping. That's what it is all about…Living and dreaming.

Today, I sleep in my own bed. I don't have roaches or mice in my home. I am no longer beaten, abused and failing in school. I earned a Ph.D. years ago. I've written and published 7 books with 6 of them becoming national bestsellers. I am happy, and I still dream. Take my story as a lesson that "you just never know." Don't give up. Don't give in and don't give away your gifts. Use them to empower you to make the positive difference in your life and in turn; it will make a difference in the lives of others. I did.

You just never know.
You just never know.

Lesson: Always "trust and believe" because you just never know.
(*Portions of this message are reprinted from Dr. Adair's first book "Go Hard and Stumble Softly…")

Day 18

"The End. Period."

Creating life lesson plans that help shape our lives helps us to realize what we need to do in order get what we want. We also learn that if things do not fit the scheme we have created, we must end it. I like to compare it to a teacher creating lesson plans for the students. Typically there are specific behavioral objectives/goals presented and then the teacher designs activities to reach those goals. The teacher attempts to adhere to the activities because all of them serve a purpose, and the teacher knows that if it does not serve a purpose, then they do not need it.

Hmmmm…

What if we applied this same philosophy to things and people in our lives? What if we created strategies and activities that were specifically aligned with our goals? What if we diminished those factors that prohibited us from reaching our dreams? Supposed we learned how to live with Lupus so that we could achieve our dreams?

Hmmmm…

To accomplish this, you have to learn how to release those things that do not serve a purpose. You have to learn how to END the relationships and situations that are not aligned with your dreams. Using the main tenets of my BELIEVE system helps you to determine what needs to be ended in your life so you can achieve your happiness regardless of whatever you have been through in your life.

Learning how to end the things that cause you pain.
Learning how to end the things that are not good for you.
Learning how to figure out what is good for you.
Learning how to determine what you don't need and what doesn't work for you.
Learning how to end the toxic relationships in your life.
Learning how to end the toxic feelings you have inside of you.
Learning how to end things that you should have never started.

Learning how to BEGIN with the END in mind.

This is just the beginning of the transformation of your thought process. It is life transforming, and it requires a paradigm shift in the way you have been approaching your life. It requires you to take a look at the life that you are leading and how you are leading it. It demands that you no longer put Band-Aids on gunshot wounds and instead, learn how to do the surgery so you can live an enriched and fulfilled life despite your heartache and pain.

I know you can travel to your destiny of happiness, and I know you can do this because you are a warrior and a survivor. You have to tools you need to live in your purpose, persist in your passion and prepare for prosperity. I believe in YOU, and I know that you can Get Over It! You just have to trust and BELIEVE.

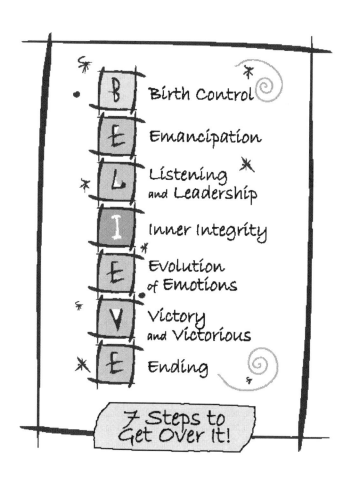

B Birth Control
E Emancipation
L Listening and Leadership
I Inner Integrity
E Evolution of Emotions
V Victory and Victorious
E Ending

7 Steps to Get Over It!

Day 19

"Mama Moment"

You know, I don't have kids who make straight A's.
Actually, one of them struggles daily just to make C's.

School is just hard for him even though he works his butt off.

And I don't have kids who get it right all the time.
They sometimes forget their manners.
They sometimes make poor choices.
They sometimes have smart a** mouths.
And they sometimes stink.
But you know what?

I have boys who are diligent, courageous, loving, responsible, hardworking, conscientious and "good" kids.

We teach them every day that it is more important for them to be "good" men then it is for them to get straight A's (but we'll take those too).

We don't raise our children to be "winners" in races that really won't matter for them in the long run of their lives.

Instead, we teach them to be the champion of who you are and be true to the core of what you represent.

Sometimes I wish others could understand our perspective and know that having "perfect" children is not our goal at all...

And if you met any of them you'll know exactly what I am talking about...

Now here is what else I think about this:

I truly believe that sometimes as parents we place the burden of our own dreams on the backs of our children. I think that we often want "more" for our kids than we may have wanted for ourselves, but we define the "more" by our own standards. The expectation, however, is that our children meet those standards.

Are you with me?

So here's my challenge…

Why are we allowing our dreams to become deferred and then pass those same dreams down to our children?

Why are we becoming slaves in bondage to our unfulfilled dreams?

Why are we not "working our dreams to live our dreams?"

So many times we reach a certain point in our lives when we just "give up" and convince ourselves that it is no longer okay to dream and create plans to achieve those dreams. Instead, it is easier for us to remain in our comfortable misery than it is to strive for that uncomfortable happiness.

We do it because we are afraid.

We do it because we are worried.

We do it because we say the dream for us no longer makes sense.

And we do it because we say the dream is just not practical anymore.

So we pass it on to our children and expect them to live up to the dreams we never fulfilled.

Our sons will be the greatest sports player ever. Or President Obama.

Our daughters will be the next Dr. Mae Jennings, Oprah Winfrey or Dr. Maya Angelou.

Because we dreamed of being the "greatest" and it didn't work out so now, we've passed that dream down to our kids.

But let me tell you something, dreams are not genetic, and they cannot be inherited.

Our children have their own dreams.

Their own ideas.

Their own passion for living in their purpose.

And I think it becomes our responsibility to help them travel along the path that God has created just for them.

Not to detour them on a path that we created for ourselves.

Dreams do not come with a warranty or a guarantee, so it is our responsibility to work our dreams to live our dreams.

No matter how old we are.

No matter how hard it gets.

No matter about the "coulda, woulda and shoulda's" in our lives.

We have to do it.

We need to do it.

Because our dreams belong to us, and we should not allow ourselves to become enslaved to fear, confusion and doubt.

We can't let previous pain predict our paths.

And create our dreams on the backs of our children.

We have to love ourselves enough to believe that we can live a life full of passion, promise, and purpose. We need to believe that we have the tenacity and courage to follow the steps that God ordered for us long ago.

And know that if our Faith remains intact, then we will still know that "what is for us, is for us" because God said so.

It's not for our children....He gave them their own dreams and their own paths to follow. So when I say to you that I embrace that my kids don't make straight A's, and one of them struggles to make C's, I am saying to you that I accept them for who they are. They are God's children, and because he chose me to be their mother while they are here on earth, I am going to take care of them with their dreams…not mine.

In this process, they will learn the critical things in life to help them maneuver through the trials and tribulations that are married to success, and they will be better and stronger because of it.

I love my children.

I love their promise.

I love their purpose.

And I love their dreams.

Because of this, I will continue to be that "foot soldier" parent emerging through the trenches to help guide them along their personalized path of life. But at the same time, I am still living in my own dream…

That's called "parenting."

Lesson: Create your own dreams for you and do not expect your children to follow them.

Action for Change

What are your 3 dreams today?

1. _____

_____

_____

_____

_____

2. _____

_____

_____

_____

_____

3. _____

_____

_____

_____

_____

_____

Day 20

I had an abortion.

Over my lifetime, several of them.

Hmmmm….

Yes, I terminated my pregnancies when I knew that I was going to give birth to negativity, doubt, self-hatred and a demolition of dreams.

When faced with the choices of giving life to these feelings or walking them to death's door, I chose the latter.

I had abortions.

You see, terminating the life of negative toxins, negative people and negative situations in your life can only give you hope, strength, and self-empowerment.

It can provide new philosophical, ideological and spiritual stances that will propel you towards prosperity.

And allow you to move forward in your life to fulfill your dreams.

I am not sorry that I ended the pregnancies that could have caused me to destroy my dreams, halt my hopes and stagnate my strength.

Sometimes we hold on to the things that hurt us the most because we are afraid to let them go, we are terrified of what our lives would be like without them, and we are scared of creating a future that does not include them.

So we impregnate ourselves with the thoughts that they are necessary and required.

And we remain pregnant with blessing blockers for a lifetime…Never allowing ourselves to give birth to our passion, our purpose, and our persistence.

We wallow in pity about the inability to fulfill our dreams.

And we waddle when we walk because we are weighted down with hurt and pain, so we are never able to walk upright with pride and perseverance.

At some point we all need abortions.

We all need to terminate any pregnancy that inflicts heartache, perpetuates powerlessness, embraces disenfranchisement and destroys dreams.

We need clarity about which relationships work for us and which people are just toxic in our lives.

What are the venoms in our daily world that seek to poison us? Find them and get rid of them.

Deciding to have an abortion is not about thinking and feeling selfishly; It's about living a productive and healthy life.

Protecting oneself.
Rebuilding oneself.
Recreating oneself.
Improving oneself.
Reclaiming oneself.

You see if we continue to impregnate ourselves with things that only serve as barriers to our mission, we will only give birth to more heartache and pain that are cloaked in blankets of shame and doubt.

We will never reach a level of positivity required for prosperity if we always bathe in our own dirt of despair and fail to lean on our shields of Grace, Faith, and Mercy.

We will always embrace elements that threaten our ability to empower ourselves because we are pregnant with hopelessness.

So I decided to have abortions.

And I really do not care what the "right-wing" has to say.

It's my life, and I have the right to choose.

I chose to have many abortions to rid myself of heartache, pain, blockers, shame and doubt.

And I will choose to have many more if anything attempts to invade my body, my heart, and my soul.

I will terminate whatever threatens the core of my existence, limits my possibilities and does not serve as an anchor for my abilities.

And will have the courage to stand in the conviction of my choice.

So yes, I had an abortion, and I am okay with it because my life is fulfilled, enriched, and empowered and I am emancipated and liberated from the shackles of self-destruction in prisons of emotional hell.

Most of all, I am happy because I choose to be "pro-life."

Lesson: Choose what you are going to be "pro-choice" about and do not be afraid to terminate any pregnancy that will only birth to negativity.

Action for Change

List 2 things that you need to "abort" in your life:

1. _____

_____

_____

_____

_____

_____

_____

_____

2. _____

_____

_____

_____

_____

_____

_____

_____

_____

**WHAT
HAPPENS
TO A
DREAM
DEFERRED?
NOTHING.
ABSOLUTELY
NOTHING.**

**WORK
YOUR
DREAM
SO YOU
CAN LIVE
YOUR
DREAM**

Lesson. Dreams don't come with a warranty or guarantee so you have to "make" it happen not just "let" it happen.

Day 21

"What If?"

(Excerpt of speech given at Daemen College Convocation, 2015)

What if we allowed ourselves to dream about the seemingly impossible?
What if we gave ourselves permission to believe in those dreams?
And what if we allowed our Faith to be stronger than our fears?
What could we accomplish?
What could we do?
How far could we go in our lives?

I want to share with you a bit about what it will take to believe in the infinite possibilities of that question "What if?" Here are 3 lessons that you must know to answer the question "What if?"

Allow yourself to dream.
Allow yourself to learn.
Give yourself permission to ask for help.
Allow yourself to Dream

I absolutely LOVE to write. I've written about 7 books, and they all focus on the concept that we have to allow ourselves to have Faith and to Dream in order to be successful. I am sure that many of you have heard of Langston Hughes, a literary genius who wrote the poem, "What happens to a Dream Deferred?" Well, my response has been "Nothing." "Absolutely Nothing." Because you shouldn't let it happen. I believe that if you "work a dream to live a dream" then it will never be deferred.

You see, dreams aren't just made for sleeping. They are your motivation and the GPS for your future. And if you allow them to become deferred, the dream becomes a nightmare.

YOU are responsible for doing the work that is required to fulfill your dreams and to utilize everything that helps you to make them come true because dreams do not come with a warranty or guarantee.
Because of this, never limit your possibilities because you will disable your abilities.

And don't allow difficulties determine your destiny.

You see, your dreams serve as the pathway to your purpose and can be used to prepare you for the prosperity that you are destined to have.

But you first have to *Allow yourself to Dream*.

Use everything around you to help you to "work your dream to live your dream" and then your dream cannot and will not be deferred.

So the next time you read the Langston Hughes poem and answer it, your response will be "Nothing!" because you will not let it happen. And when you finish one dream, you will start working on the next one.

Allow yourself to learn.

When I first arrived on my undergraduate college campus as a wide-eyed and naïve 16-year-old, I thought I knew so much because I had gone through so much in my life before I even stepped foot on the campus. I thought that I had it all figured out, and all that I needed from college was the textbook knowledge so that I could move on to the next phase of my life.

I was so wrong.

Before I "cracked the code" and realized that there was so much more that college had to teach me beyond my books, I had already begun to stagnate my growth by holding on to old thoughts, and behaviors. But once I allowed myself to absorb the full life that college had to offer, I knew that I was truly growing as a person and that no matter what I had been through in my life before attending college, I was going to be okay.

Allowing myself to learn organically and transform my way of thinking helped me to embrace the fact that I was not "special" because I had "been through" stuff in my life before coming to college so I could not allow myself to use that as an excuse to just "give up" and "walk away" from my dream.

Allowing myself to learn taught me to about diversity, spirituality, consequences and flexibility. These lessons were learned through direct experiences that I had on campus.

I learned to live and work with others from various ethnicities and cultures.

I learned how to be a bit more flexible in the way I viewed the world from many professors and the content of my courses.

And I didn't just "give up" and "walk away" when I received consequences for my actions. Instead, I figured out how to accept my consequences but still "work my dream to live my dream."

You see, when you allow yourself to learn you are allowing yourself to grow, to improve and to become a stronger person.

Be sure to have all of the support systems in place to help you to make the necessary transitions to allow yourself to learn.

Give Yourself Permission to ask for help.

Sometimes I think that we believe that we are stronger than we really have to be, and we try to do so many things alone. That's not just in college; that's in life. Well, it doesn't have to be that way. You can have the support networks you need to lead and guide you towards success.

Allow yourself to be loved, to be supported, and to be helped.

Just because you ask for help doesn't mean that you are weak…It just means that you need help.

Give yourself permission to ask for help because you need it…not because you are weak. Let me share with you a short story about this:

I remember really wanting a pair of shoes that I knew I didn't have the "extra" money to buy. I watched these shoes for several months…I would often put them in my online shopping cart but never made it to the checkout. I then watched as they went on sale, and the inventory decreased…

Oh noooo!!!! They won't have my size when I am ready to buy!

A couple of months later and the shoes were still not quite in my budget but at 70% off I knew this would be my last chance to buy them…

But how would I do this? How could I make it work?

I discovered that all I had to do all along was to "ask."

Now I'm not talking about asking God for help or praying to Jesus for a "blessing" to buy them.

I'm saying that sometimes we just need to ask for help from the people that love us.

This extends beyond my desire for a pair of shoes – it applies to our entire lives.

Sometimes we just have to let people help us.

We have to let them love us.

We have to let them do things for us that will make us happy.

For me, I've struggled with allowing others to help me. As with many of you, I suffer from the "Superwoman Syndrome."

You know, the disease that makes you believe that you can be all things to all people all the time?

The one that forces you to be the last one asleep but the first one awake each day to ensure that the household runs smoothly?

You know, the woman who is the "go-to lady" who fixes all the problems of everyone, but often forgets about herself?

Sound familiar?
Well, that's me.
Well, I should say that "used to be me."

But I've learned that it is okay to accept love and help from others. It doesn't mean that I am a loser or a quitter.

It just means that I need help.

I've learned that sometimes by letting others help me, they are helping themselves and in turn that makes me feel good.

You see, sometimes I think we overburden ourselves with feelings of Omnipotence--- as though we can do it all.

We forget that there is only one God, and only he is invincible and can conquer the world.

We get caught up in the human struggle for significance and won't allow ourselves to accept that we cannot do it all.

That we need help.
And then we are afraid to ask for the help.

We let our Fear paralyze our Faith, and we begin to think that if we are not the lone soldier emerging from the trenches, then we are not warriors.

Wrong.

We need to let others be a part of our process…a part of our pain and a part of our progress.

We need to let them love us. Help us.

And sometimes they need to love us the best way they know how…
Just because you need something or someone doesn't mean that you are "needy."
Just because you need help doesn't mean that you are "helpless."

And just because you may depend on receiving help to accomplish something does not make you a "dependent."

Although we own the power of change, that doesn't mean that we have to change it alone.

Sometimes we just have to accept that we need someone to help us.
And then we just have to ask.

Amazing, after months of pondering about this particular pair of shoes a "light bulb" went off in my head, and I realized how I could solve this "problem."

I simply had to ask for help.

Now some of you are probably saying that this is so trivial, and if I couldn't afford the shoes then, I probably shouldn't get them anyway…

I get that. I understand that. And I know that.

But my point is that if I couldn't find the "strength" to ask for help just for a pair of shoes then how would I find the "strength" to ask for help with more significant things in my life? How would I ever begin to let go of some of the perceived power I thought I needed? How would I learn to "let go" of some of the "pseudo" control?

Hmmmmm….
I learned I had to start somewhere…
And for me, it began with the shoes.
Knowing that it was okay to ask for help when I needed it was a big step and transition for me, and I lifted many burdens from my shoulders over the years.

I now let people love me.
I now let people help me.
And I now "Let Go and Let God" because I know I cannot do it alone…

This story is greater than a pair of shoes that I wanted…It was about learning to ask for help when I needed it. And to accept help when it is offered. It was about learning to let others love you. Learning to let others help you. And still knowing that your pride, dignity, and faith are all still intact. You lose nothing. And you gain everything. Help. Ask for it.

So What If you actually believed the words that I just shared with you?

What if you knew that:
Your Faith is stronger than your Fear so you should not be afraid to dream.
You are already equipped and empowered.
You are already promised and prepared.
You already have permission to persevere.

What if you knew that If you start before you are ready, and then when it is your time, you will already be ready?

And what if you knew that you should learn to make adjustments, and not excuses?
Hmmm…
What if you actually knew all of this?

Let me share a very short story.

Last year I went to a track competition, and I watched 8-year-olds begin the 1500 meter race and they were so energized and excited at the start. I watched the kids as they ran around the track a couple of times but by the third lap the gap between the lead runner and the last runner was pretty significant. I saw the struggle, pain and desperation in the faces of the kids as they ran. I saw some tears, and I watched many of them as they struggled to finish the race. This may be parallel to a life journey.

Many of you wake up each morning eager and excited. You are ready to run this life race, but you have no idea how tired you will get, how rough it can be and how much you may struggle. You don't know how this race is going to end but right now, today, you feel ready to begin the race.

Just like the 8-year-olds who discovered the depth of their resiliency, you will find yourself doing the same thing in life. But if you follow the 3 lessons that I shared with you (allow yourself to dream, allow yourself to learn and give yourself permission to ask for help). And if you do this, you will also cross that finish line and know that you are the "victor" claiming the "victory" in this race called "Life."

Action for Change

**Think about the 3 lessons I taught in my ""What If?" speech.
Which lesson do you think will apply to your life first? Why?**

_____

_____

_____

_____

_____

_____

_____

_____

_____

_____

_____

_____

_____

_____

_____

_____

_____

_____

The following messages and lessons are reprints from previous books but are the most popular and most requested...Enjoy!

"I Won't Forgive..."

One of the hardest things that I've I had to do in my life was to forgive someone who hurt me.

Someone who hurt me to the core...

Who lit a flame of pain in my spirit and lit a match to my soul?

My heart was on fire because of how I was treated and how badly I was hurting because of this person.

I remember that I couldn't eat...I would raise the fork to my mouth, open my mouth, put the food in my mouth and then couldn't chew.

I felt that I had no energy to eat because all of my energy had been saturated and drained with the hurt.

And "that person" did it to me.

I couldn't sleep...tossing and turning for many nights trying to make the memory of that person disappear and devising ways to get back at them...

To make them hurt as I hurt...

To feel as I did.

To know heartache as I was feeling it...

Yes, I had it bad...I hurt so much so how could I even begin to Get Over It! and begin to forgive that person?

I began by first forgiving myself for allowing me to be in that situation...

There were signs, but I chose not to read them.

Yes, I saw the signs, but I made the decision not to read them.

I had to forgive myself for making poor decisions.

I also learned that I wouldn't be able to forgive anyone or anything if I didn't strengthen my faith in God.

That if I didn't believe in his ultimate power to lead me through the pain then I would never be able to forgive truly.

So I began to lean consistently on my shield of faith more frequently and depend on my prayers being answered for that much-needed strength.

After that, I began allowing myself to heal and then forgiving myself for getting into that situation in the first place.

Only by first healing myself was I able to begin the process of forgiving the other person.

You see, I was no longer angry, hurt and confused.

My heart is now pumped at a normal pace when I thought of that person and situation.

I knew that forgiving them was a process, and it began by praying for them.

Wrapping them in my prayers daily and asking God to inject my spirit with more compassion and understanding.

Forgiving them was the final step in my own healing process, and I knew that the only way for me to truly move forward and to Get Over It! was to forgive them.

Walking that long, uncomfortable road of forgiveness is challenging but required if we want to heal our inner pain.

It's needed if we want to free ourselves from the jail of hurt that we feel we've been sentenced to.

It's required to liberate ourselves from the emotional enslavement to the mistakes of the past.

We have to write our own proclamation of freedom through the forgiveness of others...

This is the only way to 100% let them go.

And, it's the heart of what it means to be a Christian.

Yes, I know that it's hard to forgive others, and it does take time, energy and efforts that we think we don't have, but it is necessary.

If we don't then the hurt never really goes away...

It emerges each time we see a person who hurt us and every time we think about the situation.

You can't put Band-Aids on gunshot wounds and expect it to heal.

All it will do is become infected and compromise the rest of your body.

It will fester and eventually release toxins that can stagnate your personal growth.

So you have to go in and do the surgery on that wound and then stitch it up so you can fully heal...

Forgiving others is that surgery, and you'll need it to move forward in your life and your relationships with others.

I did it.

I performed surgeries in my life...not once or twice but numerous times...

I needed to.

I had to.

So I did.

It was the only way for me to Get Over It! so I could live again...

Forgiveness is hard but living in a world of heartache, and inner pain is harder... Choose to forgive.

Lesson: If you don't forgive those who may have hurt you then you are sentencing yourself to a jail filled with anger, resentment, and hurt...There's no "get out jail free card" for this kind of pain. Learn to let it go and begin the process of forgiveness.

"This Manual..."

Sometimes there are just some things that don't come in that manual called life...

You're left just to figure it out yourself.

But that doesn't mean that you can't ask for help

Or pray for guidance.

It just means that the answer may not be laid out in front of you with a plate, knife, fork, and spoon.

You see, you may get damaged, but that doesn't mean you are destroyed

And your heart may feel discouraged, but that doesn't mean it is defeated.

Your soul may be a bit tattered, but it's not torn

And those blisters on your toes are not really wounded; they're just throbbing from those painful shoes you may have worn.

Sometimes your vision may appear to be cloudy, but you're not really blind

Because when you really push through the pain, those hurtful sights are left behind.

And we know that our faith is often tested

But we also know that if we seek, trust and believe, we are never rejected.

And oh, our backs where we carry our burdens are often so sore,

But our inner strength and positive energy that God has given us always allow us to handle just a little more.

All of the pressure and the stress has not broken us yet.

But sometimes our approaches to these rough situations won't let us forget.

There is no one perfect way to live our lives

But remaining in a good frame of mind is step one out of the negativity and strife.

We need to remember not to "borrow worries" and to walk the other way

And to sometimes really get down on our knees to pray

For me, it has made a difference in the ways I cope

And reminds me that even in tragedy there is a triumph, in the loss there is a gain, in death there is life and in despair there is hope.

I try to live surrounded by peace and harmony.

Because I know no matter how challenging my life gets my faith, and my God are walking through it right with me.

Lesson: If faith can move mountains then it can move you too. No matter how bad things get in your life, and you feel like you've lost it all, NEVER, EVER let go of your faith...That's the one thing that no one can take away from you...You can only lose it yourself.

"Work it Baby..."

If it doesn't feel uncomfortable or it doesn't hurt then you are probably not trying your hardest.

If you are not second-guessing your next move then, you are probably not doing new things.

If you already know the answers to your own questions, then you've probably been in the same place for a long time.

And if your dreams only appear at night then you've probably lost some faith in becoming "more" than what you already are.

You see to make changes in our lives we must think differently to act differently.

And we must feel different to do different things.

We own the power of change.

And we possess the strength to make a change.

We just have to do the work to do it.

Push ourselves through our own self-imposed limits...

Force ourselves to have paradigm shifts ---altering our perspectives of the world.

Allowing ourselves fo approach life and situations from a new angle.

Teaching ourselves to walk up a mountain with the same tenacity that we have when we run down the hill.

Knowing that if we feel comfortable in our current life then we haven't made changes.

That perhaps we haven't required ourselves to define our destiny.

Or we have limited our possibilities.

You see, pushing ourselves to our breaking points is not supposed to be easy...

We pushing for a "break-through" and not a "break-down."

We are supposed to feel our own transformations...

Those changes within ourselves for ourselves.

And just because it doesn't feel good doesn't make it bad...It just means that your soul is working, and that change is taking place.

It's the time when we learn that if we know better, then we will do better...

And if we do better; then we become better for ourselves.

Yes, if you don't feel it then you are probably not working hard enough...

And if you are not working hard enough then you really should ask yourself if you wanted "it" at all to begin with...

Lesson: Achieving your optimal level of success can be a painful process --- You may shed some tears and sweat it out, but that's just a normal part of the journey to reach your highest level of performance...Prepare yourself for this workout and know that anything worth having should also be worth fighting and sweating for...You need this to "Get Over It, Get Through It and Keep it Moving."

"The SWOT of Me"

Sometimes we look in the mirror, and we don't recognize the person staring back at us. Sort of like a reflection of a person who never really was.

And there are times in our lives when we "lose" ourselves and forget our self-worth because we are caught up living another life that really doesn't define us.

It may be those times when we are actually chasing rainbows that don't have pots of gold at the end of them that we realize that it was just "fool's gold" all along…

Perhaps it is at those moments that we need to evaluate our lives to determine what our strengths, weaknesses, opportunities and threats are.

Strengths focus on what we are good at and the good things in our lives…those things that can inspire us and keep us dreaming and knowing that "Yes, we can!" These are the characteristics/things in our lives that can place us at an advantage over us to help others to achieve our goals.

Weaknesses are the exact opposite of our strengths because these are the characteristics/things that slow our growth and development. These qualities/ obstacles or stumbling blocks can prohibit us from developing into positive beings and submerges our productive thoughts and activities under a concrete slab of negativity. What type of waste is in your life now? What are your weaknesses that you are aware of? Who are the "weak" people that you allow to remain in your life? What are your consistent weak moments?

Opportunities focus on those external chances that you may receive to make a positive difference in your life. How many times have you passed on an opportunity because of doubt or fear? I think we miss good opportunities in our lifetimes because we have a fear of the unknown and the fear of failure. We would rather live in a "comfortable hell" (as my friend Tre says) than reach out and take a chance in an "uncomfortable heaven." We often get too comfortable in our skin and our environments that we live in a victim's mentality and will not seize the opportunity to move toward positive change in our lives. If you are going to Get Over It! then you have to take advantage of some of the opportunities that may come your way. You see, there will be people who offer you a chance but it is your responsibility to accept the opportunity. That's what opportunity is all about.

God can definitely bless you with talent, but if you don't take the opportunity to "grow" the talent, then it is basically a talent wasted. As you continue to work on your self-directed search, don't forget to take advantage of some opportunities along the way.

Threats…Be wary of these because they represent those challenges to your opportunities, dreams and to your sanity. These are the external elements that can threaten your progress and seek to destroy your dreams. You need to be prepared at all times for those elements and those people who only wish the worst for you.

Be wary of yourself too, sometimes we can be our own worst enemy because we live in that comfortable hell and will threaten our own reality… So as we stare in that mirror and gaze into those eyes and we are struggling to get a glimpse of that soul inside, we need to remove those layers of pain, lift the veil of heartache, so there is nothing left to hide. We don't need to focus on what "coulda, woulda, shoulda" been but simply wasn't… But we can begin to accept and work on what really is. So who is that person staring at us, who could it be? Those eyes look like mine but is it really ME?

Lesson: To Thine Own Self Be True

(Shakespeare, http://www.enotes.com/hamlet-text/act-i-scene-iii#ham-1-3-82)

"I'm Not Gon' Hurt Anymore"

If someone is hurting you then why do you want them in your life?

If someone is abusing you then why would you need them in your life?

If someone is consistently lying to you then what is the purpose of them in your life? Hmmmm....

These are questions that you have to answer from deep within yourself. You have to dig deep, face the truth and deal with the issues within yourself that allow you to accept these people in your life.

I don't think that we intentionally place a "welcome mat" at the front door of our lives to invite negativity in. But some of us become that "provocative victim" where we play games and start things that we have no intention of finishing, and we build relationships that we knew were unhealthy from the start, and then we wonder "what happened?"

We see the signs way ahead that direct us to make the right turn out of the relationship, but yet we still drive straight ahead into the abusive and negative situation because we are searching for a love/relationship that may never exist with this person. Or, we keep trying to "change" that family member because we think they are supposed to love us in a certain way just because "we are family." And then we are the ones hurt. We feel betrayed. We feel lost. And we feel confused.

You see, most relationships make you feel that way sometimes anyway, but it's when it becomes consistently unhealthy that we must learn just to walk away. We must learn that when it's time to go. It's just time to go. Whether it's the relationships, we have with our significant others, family, friends or even supervisors. If it hurts us worse than it soothes us, then we have to question why we really need it in our lives.

Sometimes people love us the best the way they know how and then we try to change that love and train that love in order to breed a new love. But that just doesn't work either.

We can't control how people love us...just how we accept that love.

You own the power of change so you can change who you allow to love you,

And if it hurts really bad, just let it go.

Take yourself through the mourning and healing process of letting them go out of your life.

Love them differently now or don't love them at all.

Love yourself more and know when you've had enough.

Yes, hurt hurts.

That's what it is supposed to do.

But letting go releases "stuff" and that's what it is supposed to do...

So let go of the hurt, lies, and emotional, psychological and/or physical abuse that may encircle a relationship that you are in. Let go of that negative relationship you may have with your own self because sometimes we hurt ourselves more than anyone else is capable of.

I could go on and on, but it's simple...Know when it is time to "walk away." And know when it is time to "Let go and Let God."

Lesson: Examine the relationships in your life and own that power of change to determine which relationship you need to walk away from.

"Running Around in Circles"

Have you ever seen a dog chase its own tail?

They go around and around, and they look pretty crazy hunh?

And then we wonder why they do it.

Well, as humans we do the same thing.

We spin ourselves in circles by doing the same wrong things over and over again.

They're called bad habits, and we often do them because it's easier.

Easier to live in a "comfortable hell" then to strive for life in an "uncomfortable heaven."

And then we think we are "happy."

Hmmmm... So at what point do we stop and begin to make a change?

To break the cycle of self-destruction and perhaps self-inflicted pain?

What will it take to allow ourselves to let the negativity in our lives and the bad habits go? Hmmmm...

The difference between humans and dogs is that we simply have a greater degree of ownership.

We know better so we can do better and we own the power of choice and change to make a difference.

Use it.

Lesson: Where is your tail? Are you chasing it or, are you in control of it?

"It Just Didn't Work Out!"

Sometimes Life just doesn't work the way we want it to...no matter how hard we try.

Sometimes Love just doesn't work the way we want it to...no matter how much we give. Sometimes Friendships just don't work out...no matter how much we trusted in them. Sometimes Jobs just don't last as long as we want and need them to...no matter how much time and energy we put into them.

The loss of Life, Love, Friendships and Jobs can be devastating to our hearts and souls, but your commitment and faith to YOURSELF should never waver.

You know that God orders your steps, and you will follow that rocky path he has set forth for you because you understand that it is really just your stepping stone to greatness. You know you won't let any disabilities disable your abilities.

And you know that you will still smile after any of these losses because you still have Faith and somehow, someway, it will work out.

You own the spirit of positivity and the power of change so you will begin the process of moving forward.

Nothing will stop you.

Yes, "stuff" happens and it hurts real badly, but you have the strength and faith in your soul to remain a "believer" and know that your new tomorrow actually begins today.

We all go through "stuff" in our lives, and we are not "special" because of it so we shouldn't feel as though we deserve a "pass" in our world because we are "hurting."

Instead, we should stock up on our ammunition so we can come out "shooting" with positive moves each time we are hurting, and we can destroy the negativity aimed our way... So, let's start our day by "Getting over it, Getting through it and Keeping it moving."

Lesson: Get Over It, Get Through It and Keep It Moving....

"I am not ashamed..."

There have been some things in my life that I probably should have just walked away from.

Certain situations, certain people and certain things

But I made that conscientious decision to stay.

Stay to fight for it.

Stay to believe in it.

Stay to trust in it.

And stay because I just felt "I needed to."

I really didn't look at it as right or wrong...

It was what it was, and I did what I had to do.

I did what I knew best and when I knew better I did better.

That's the power of resiliency.

We lean on our shields of hope to help us get through tough times

And we rely on our hearts to guide us in the right direction.

But what about our Faith?

At what point are do we open the windows of our souls to allow Faith to breeze into our lives?

When do we give credit to the sweet spirit of God performing his miracles in our lives?

For understanding that it was God's will the entire time that permitted us to stay in situations, things and with some people that everyone else thought we should have given up on?

Now don't get me wrong. I'm not saying that it was God's grace that authorized abuse in your life or the Devil's work on your daily existence.

But it has been through the steps that he has ordered for you that you found the audacity of hope, dreams and the tenacity cloaked by the courage to keep fighting for what you believed in.

Sometimes it's God's whisper that has the loudest voice around us, and we must be still to hear it.

We must silence all anguish, doubt, fear, shame, confusion, sadness, frustration, denial, despair and negative attitudes to hear the voice of God speaking directly to us. Silence people and things around you and you will feel God's direct message to you.

So when I tell you that I stood firm in certain situations, things and with certain people I am saying this because I heard my God's words speaking to me.

I felt his presence in my decisions because I consulted him.

I asked for his guidance and asked for him to wrap his arms around me and hold me tight as I made difficult choices in my life.

To nourish my starving and confused heart and mind with the nutrients of obedience, self-love, and self-empowerment so I could believe in my choices and know that failure has never been an option in my life.

And were my decisions always right?

Hmmmm....

I am a happy, healthy and spirit-filled woman right now, today, at this very moment so I would say YES!

Were my decisions "easy" to live with just because I had God on my side?

NO!

But it was easier to live with myself knowing I made my choice with God on my side.

You see, it's all about faith for me.

All about remembering that if faith the size of a mustard seed can move a big ol' mountain then it would have no problem moving me too.

I trust.

I believe.

And know that at the end of the day when it is only me lying in the bed with my thoughts that I know I have to love me and live the rest of my life with any decisions that I've made...

But I can do it because the windows to my soul are always open, and the breezes of God and faith are always blowing in my direction.

And, it feels good. Damn good.

Lesson: Breezes are always blowing...whether you open your windows or not. Choose to leave them open. "Fresh" air can be soooo good for you.

"My Faith Moves My Mountains"

It's funny how just when we think we are "over" something or someone it only takes one instance to remind us that we are not.

When your heart is broken, there is not a surgery that can piece it back together to its original form.

There will always be the stitches to show how it was repaired and then the scar to remind you of the wound.

And the time it takes to heal is never known because each hurt is so different and the depth and breadth of the hurt changes with each situation.

It's scary to think that you are "over it" and then you realize that it still hurts.

So what can you do?

Hmmmm...Probably not much at all.

Buttttt....We can always try.

We don't always own the power of love and pain.

We can't help who we love, and we can only limit our pain, but we are going to feel.

That's what makes us uniquely human.

And when we sometimes feel, that brings us pain.

But we can lean on our shield of Faith and know that tomorrow is just a day away.

That after the rain the sun eventually comes out.

That after the winter the Spring always comes.

That after the complex twists and turns in the road there will be a straightaway coming up, that after dipping deep in the valley of despair we will start climbing up the hills and mountains to reach our happy places.

That after the labor pains there is a birth that will remind us of the wonder of life. That after teaching there is a lesson learned.

That after hard work there is always time to play and that after we have drained our minds/bodies of self-made positivity, then our faith is there to replenish us.

So you see, although there are some things that we may NEVER get over in our lives we can still get through them.

While we can't necessarily control who we love or when we hurt, we can control the effect it can have on our lives.

Having Faith helps us to know that the hurt will soon be filled with the happy, and the pain will be swapped out for pleasure.

Faith does that for you.
Yes, hurt hurts.
And we want it to go away.

I absolutely hate it when it comes back...that "surprise bumping-into" meeting, the old photo that you come across, a song you hear and simple birthday that you remember can stir those emotions that cause you to hurt.

You just never know what will trigger these feelings. But what you can hold on to is that your Faith will pull you through it all.

I've said this many times, and I'm going to say it again here....

Faith is a miraculous healer.
It's a "mover" and a "shaker."

If Faith the size of a mustard seed can move mountains, then it can surely move you.

Know it.
Keep it.
Empower and embrace yourself in it.
Love yourself for believing in it.

Lesson: You can't always control your pain, but you can always have faith that you will get through it.

Conclusion

So there you have it, 21 Days of TRUTH to help you push through your pain, inspire your dreams, motivate your actions and empower your purpose. I hope that reading these messages will help you to change your mindset because you must first change the way you think before you can change the way you behave. The words I share with you in this book is a start….I cannot guarantee the type of difference the messages will make in your life because dreams don't come with a warranty or a guarantee.

You must "work a dream to live a dream" and it begins with changing the way you think. Begin to think about your life differently. Begin to think about your purpose differently. And begin to think about who you are and what you want differently. You own the power of change, and you are the starting point for the change so use it as you lean on those triple shields of Grace, Faith, and Mercy for strength.

Journal Pages

Use these pages to write your thoughts and ideas as you reflect during these twenty-one days.

About the Author

Dr. White-johnson is the author of "Go Hard and Stumble Softly" published in July, 2012 and "Get Over It! 7 Steps to Live Well with Lupus." She is also the author of "Get Over It! How to Bounce Back after Hitting Rock Bottom," "How to Get Over It! in 30 Days" Parts I & II, "Get Over It! How to Bounce Back after Hitting Rock Bottom for Teens" and "White Girl Speaks: Powerful Words of Inspiration for Leadership and Success in Your Life!" In addition, she has created an award-winning leadership and personal development curriculum and program for teens that is aligned with the national Common Core Standards and the American School Counselor Association National Model Standards.

Her latest curriculum that focuses on Teen Dating Violence will be released in the summer of 2016. She earned her Ph.D. from the University at Buffalo and holds a master's degree in the counseling field. Dr. White-johnson is married and the mother of five children.

Contact Information

Dr. Adair f. White-johnson

@dr_adairwj

@dr_adair

Dr. Adair White-johnson

DRADAIRSPEAKS.COM

info@dradairspeaks.com or 888-400-7302

Books by Dr. Adair!

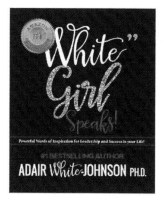